Psalm 23 is the inspiration of this devotional.
Love, protection, guidance and provision
are the promises of God,
who is faithful and true.

THE LORD IS MY SHEPHERD

The LORD is my shepherd; I shall not want.
He makes me to lie down in green pastures:
He leads me beside the still waters.
He restores my soul:
He leads me in the paths of righteousness
for His name's sake.

Yea, though I walk through
the valley of the shadow of death,
I will fear no evil:
for You are with me;
Your rod and Your staff, they comfort me.

You prepare a table before me
in the presence of my enemies:
You anoint my head with oil;
my cup runs over.
Surely goodness and mercy
shall follow me all the days of my life:
and I will dwell in the house of the LORD forever.

Psalm 23
(NKJV)

THE LORD IS MY SHEPHERD

JOURNAL ~ DIARIO

WRITTEN AND ILLUSTRATED
BY GABRIELLA EVA NAGY

ISBN 13: 978-1-61244-402-4

Printed in the United States of America

Published by Halo Publishing International
1100 NW Loop 410
Suite 700 - 176
San Antonio, Texas 78213
Toll Free 1-877-705-9647
Website: www.halopublishing.com
E-mail: contact@halopublishing.com

EL SEÑOR ES MI PASTOR

El SEÑOR es mi pastor; nada me faltará.
En lugares de delicados pastos me hará yacer,
me conduce a fuentes tranquilas, allí reparo mis fuerzas,
Confortará mi alma;
me guiará por sendas de justicia,
haciendo honor a su nombre.

Aunque pase por el más oscuro de los valles,
no temeré peligro alguno,
porque tú, SEÑOR, estás conmigo;
tu vara y tu bastón me inspirarán confianza.

Prepararas una mesa delante de mí
ante los ojos de mis enemigos;
has vertido aceite en mi cabeza,
mi copa está rebosando.
Tu bondad y tu misericordia me acompañan
todos los dás de mi vida,
y habitaré en la casa del SEÑOR moraré por largos días.

Salmo 23
(NVI)

www.ingramcontent.com/pod-product-compliance
Lightning Source LLC
LaVergne TN
LVHW071727230826
846093LV00024B/543

* 9 7 8 1 6 1 2 4 4 4 0 2 4 *